Brief Guide to Extemporaneous Public Speaking

Blake J. Neff
Scott D. Turcott

Brief Guide to Extemporaneous Public Speaking
Blake J. Neff and Scott D. Turcott

Direct correspondence and permission requests to one of the following:

E-mail: info@trianglepublishing.com
Web site: www.trianglepublishing.com
Mail: Triangle Publishing
Indiana Wesleyan University
1900 West 50th Street
Marion, Indiana 46953

The *Chicago Manual of Style* is the preferred style guide of Triangle Publishing.

Published by Triangle Publishing
Marion, Indiana 46953
Printed in the United States of America

ISBN: 978-1-931283-30-4

Cover and graphic design: Lyn Rayn

CONTENTS

INTRODUCTION

During one of the most unconventional convention speeches in the history of political gatherings, Elizabeth Dole left the platform and confidently strolled among the delegates at the Republican National Convention on August 14, 1996. Her speech supported the candidacy of her husband, Bob Dole, for President of the United States. But it wasn't the thesis or the words that made the greatest impression. It was the absence of a podium, printed notes, and a teleprompter that led observers in the San Diego hall to report that the speech seemed more like a conversation than a formal address.[1]

"'I am going to be speaking to friends, and I'm going to be speaking about the man I love. It's just a lot more comfortable for me to do this down here with you,' she said as she descended the podium steps."[2] While the speech appeared spontaneous, it was in fact a well rehearsed and carefully crafted rhetorical moment. The result was extremely effective. More than one observer noted that Dole was being "celebrated by Republicans for a politically deft and commanding performance."[3] Politics aside, the speech provides a vivid example of the impact of extemporaneous public speaking.

EXTEMPORANEOUS PUBLIC SPEAKING
Public speaking that is characterized by a well-prepared speech that is delivered with few, if any, notes.

Extemporaneous is from the Latin phrase, *ex tempore,* meaning "out of time." While the extemporaneous delivery style sometimes appears spur of the moment, it's actually very different than impromptu speaking. Extemporaneous speeches are carefully prepared and diligently practiced, then delivered with few, if any, notes. The precise word choices are selected during the process of delivery. As a result, the same speech can be given several times using different words but using the same points and structure. *Extemporaneous* applies to the words themselves that are *tempore* (or temporary) with each speaking event.

MANUSCRIPT PUBLIC SPEAKING
Public speaking that is characterized by reading a manuscript of the speech word for word.

MEMORIZED PUBLIC SPEAKING
Public speaking that is characterized by the speaker reciting the speech word for word from memory.

Alternatives to the extemporaneous style exist. The most common alternatives are reading a manuscript or memorizing the precise words of the entire speech. Still, extemporaneous speaking is what many experts view as "the ideal style of delivery"[4] that "combines the careful preparation and structure of a manuscript presentation with the spontaneity and enthusiasm of an unrehearsed talk."[5]

Brief Guide to Extemporaneous Public Speaking is based on the conviction that the benefits are well worth the extra effort required to effectively accomplish extemporaneous delivery. The guide examines:

- Advantages of extemporaneous delivery
- Challenges to extemporaneous delivery
- Preparing an extemporaneous speech
- Delivering an extemporaneous speech

At certain points, the reader will encounter brief biographies of speakers who have discovered and mastered the extemporaneous approach. Some of these biographies are of well-known historic rhetoricians. Other biographies focus on the speaking style of contemporary public speakers. Some of the subjects used the extemporaneous style exclusively. Others found it the most effective for a particular speech. Together, the accounts demonstrate that speakers in all facets of public speaking have discovered the value of extemporaneous delivery.

This guide is written primarily for beginning students of public speaking and homiletics. In these settings, it will usually be required alongside a primary public speaking text that focuses on the process of speech or sermon building. That text might even include a chapter on extemporaneous delivery. *Brief Guide to Extemporaneous Public Speaking* will, in most cases, enhance that primary text by offering an expanded view of the importance and procedure for developing an extemporaneous address.

Those who have been engaged in public speaking for some time, whether pastor, reformer, politician, or lecturer will also benefit from this guide. That's because speakers tend to develop a personal style that must be periodically reevaluated for effectiveness. The guide pilots these readers through this reassessment process.

Brief Guide to Extemporaneous Public Speaking is offered to readers with a prayerful hope that America's appetite for effective oratory will be renewed. The first step in such a renewal will undoubtedly be a return to the "ideal style of delivery."

JONATHAN EDWARDS

Jonathan Edwards was born in East Windsor, Connecticut, in 1703, the fifth of eleven children. Educated in theology and philosophy at Yale University, he became the pastor of a church in Northampton, Massachusetts, in 1726. The large and influential congregation was previously led by his grandfather, Solomon Stoddard. The widespread revivals, that later came to be known as the First Great Awakening, thrust Edwards to international fame as a revivalist preacher.

Ralph Lewis notes that Jonathan Edwards came to the extemporaneous style later in his speaking career.[1] Early on, his notoriously poor eyesight, combined with the Puritan penchant for thrift, meant that many of his manuscripts were on very tiny scraps of paper with little or no margins. As a result, it was often necessary for a young man to hold a lantern over his shoulder to provide light for reading.

Edwards later advocated either memorization or extemporaneous delivery as preferred styles for sermonizing. No one seems certain whether this shift was a result of physical necessity or a genuine discovery of the advantage of extemporaneous address. Orville Hitchcock indicates that after 1746, Edwards began to depend more on outlines than manuscripts. As more time passed, even these notes became more and more sketchy. "The outlines for some of his last sermons at Stockbridge are very incomplete. They cover little more than the main heads of the speeches."[2] Edwards would buffet these main heads with precise words that arose in the course of the delivery.

NOTES

1. Ralph Lewis, "Preaching With and Without Notes," *Handbook of Contemporary Preaching*, ed. Michael Duduit (Nashville: Broadman, 1992), 409–419.
2. Orville A. Hitchcock, "Jonathan Edwards," *History and Criticism of American Public Address*, Vol. II, ed. William Norwood Brignance, (New York: McGraw-Hill, 1943), 213–237.

1

ADVANTAGES OF EXTEMPORANEOUS DELIVERY

Speakers agree that the extemporaneous delivery style is both difficult and time consuming. Do benefits of extemporaneous speaking really outweigh the challenges? Yes. Several advantages of the style emerge and combine to demonstrate that extemporaneous delivery is indeed well worth the extra effort.

DELIVERY POWER

One of the most compelling advantages to using extemporaneous delivery lies in the fact that the style offers greater power to the speaker. This advantage becomes clear after careful analysis of the "I have a dream" speech.[1] Dr. Martin Luther King, Jr., the famous civil rights activist, delivered this speech. This seventeen-minute speech was delivered on August 28, 1963, at the Washington Mall in Washington, D.C. The audience was comprised of nearly a quarter of a million people. King was the last of a dozen civil rights leaders to speak in support of the civil rights bill proposed to Congress by President John F. Kennedy. Preliminary speakers were limited to five minutes each. King's speech was considered the keynote.

King's rhetorical strategy was twofold. In the face of calls from black Muslim leaders for more violent civil disobedience, he appealed to his followers to resist violence in their continued struggle for equality. Because these listeners did not necessarily agree with the basic nonviolent thesis of the King address, he used a reversal strategy to change their minds to favor his position.

King also used a reinforcement strategy to persuade his listeners, both black and white, to keep on for as long as necessary in the face of mounting opposition. To this group he declared that the civil rights bill would not be passed without the strong support of his audience members.

The first two-thirds of the speech reminded listeners of where they had been in the struggle. He used phrases like "fresh from narrow jail cells" and "veterans of creative suffering." It was also in this opening segment that King employed the vivid imagery of a bank draft. He reminded the audience that the founding fathers promised that all men would be granted the inalienable rights of life, liberty, and the pursuit of happiness. He maintained that America had defaulted on that promise. "We refuse to believe that the bank of justice is bankrupt," King declared.

In the last third of the speech, King revealed his vision for the future. He pictured an America where "little black boys and black girls will be able to join hands with little white boys and white girls as sisters and brothers." It is in this portion of the speech that King repeated the phrase, "I have a dream," a total of nine times.

The content of the speech has been effectively analyzed by a host of scholars from a variety of viewpoints.[2] But textual analysis tells only a small part of the story. Steven Lucas notes, "If you have heard a recording of 'I Have a Dream,' you know its impact was heightened by King's delivery."[3] In the closing segment of the speech, King switches from a formal and rigid delivery, to an extemporaneous delivery. As a result, King's eye contact increases; his energy level appears greater; he feeds off the responses of the audience; and his gesturing is more noticeable and effective.

In short, there is power in this final segment of the speech that has made it memorable for more than four decades.

Biographer Mervyn Warren quotes King as saying this about extemporaneous delivery: "Without a manuscript, I can communicate better with an audience. Further, I have greater rapport and power when I am able to look the audience in the eye."[4]

AUDIENCE RAPPORT

According to Warren, King mentioned audience rapport and power. It's not unusual for an extemporaneous speaker to recognize audience rapport as a natural byproduct of extemporaneous delivery.

Two farmers were chatting about sermons given by their new pastor. While they didn't know the word *extemporaneous*, they did know what appealed to them and what held their attention. One of the men said, "When we talk about growing soybeans or raising calves we don't need to read our ideas to one another — we just know what we're talking about." In reality, manuscript speakers and those who memorize their speeches know their subject matter just as well as an extemporaneous speaker. But audiences react to their speeches very differently. The extemporaneous speaker usually develops a more positive, natural rapport with the audience.

In a public speaking class at a university, Kara used a blended style of delivery. She had a manuscript of her introduction, her main points, and the conclusion. Several illustrations within the body of the speech were personal experiences that she was comfortable with, so she opted to deliver them extemporaneously. She later reported that when she, by means of internal signpost, switched to the extemporaneous style, the audience reaction dramatically changed. "I had no idea that the words *for example* had such power," she said. In fact, it was not those words that enlivened Kara's audience, but the fact that they knew what was to follow—an extemporaneous story.

So positive is the audience reaction to extemporaneous speaking that in at least one time and place, it became the law. Wayne McDill reports that in Bern, Switzerland, in 1667, church leaders passed the Bern Preacher Act requiring sermons to be delivered extemporaneously. The act declared that preachers engaged in sermon delivery "must not read the same in front of the congregation from notes on paper." Rationale for the requirement included that reading a speech "is a mockery to have to watch and which takes away all fruit and grace . . . in the eyes of the listeners."[5] By contrast, extemporaneous delivery builds rapport between the speaker and the audience.

INTERNAL SIGNPOST
Very brief statements that signal the audience as to where the speaker is headed in the speech.

FLEXIBLE WORDING

Only the extemporaneous style allows the speaker to select words as the speech is delivered. This freedom allows the speaker to select the most appropriate word choices for the particular speaking event.

Professional speakers will often deliver the same basic speech many times. For example, a political candidate might use a basic stump speech repeatedly during the course of a campaign. A manuscript or memorized delivery forces the candidate to use the same words with each delivery. The extemporaneous delivery, on the other hand, makes it possible to modify the words to the setting, audience, or events of the day.

Consider the hypothetical candidate running a statewide race where there are both industrial centers and agricultural areas. The candidate's economic plan has benefits for both the farmer and the factory worker. But the candidate wants to emphasize benefits to the farmer in one part of the state and the benefits for industrial workers in another setting. An extemporaneous style allows the candidate to give the same points from the same thesis across the

ABRAHAM LINCOLN

One of the best known and most revered American presidents is the sixteenth holder of the office, Abraham Lincoln. Born near Hodgenville, Kentucky, in 1809, he was raised in Indiana and rose to prominence in Illinois.

Lincoln became an avid reader at an early age, and practiced his vocabulary and elocution by speaking to the other children in the household. Biographer Louis Warren writes, "He made them his captive audience . . . In the summer months he held these sessions out-of-doors, mounting a stump and addressing Sarah and the three Johnston children as they sat on a fallen tree. Sometimes his father and Sally and Dennis Hanks and visiting neighbors would stop to listen."[1] "A cluster of tall and stately trees often made him a most dignified and appreciative audience . . ."[2]

His practiced extemporaneous style was heightened by a superb memory that served him well in his early political endeavors before the prairie voters of the 1850s. According to Mildred Berry, the delivery of Lincoln's speeches after his election to the presidency reveal a marked change. "Many factors conspired to make them compositions, superb literary efforts rather than speeches. The customs of office combined with the criticism of his colloquial language in informal remarks forced him to read from a manuscript."[3] Sadly, events deprived one of the greatest orators in American history of his chosen style.

NOTES

1. Louis A. Warren, *Lincoln's Youth: Indiana Years Seven to Twenty-one 1816–1830* (Indianapolis: Indiana Historical Society, 1991), 80.
2. Henry Steele Commager, *Herndon's Life of Lincoln* (New York: Da Capo, 1983), 40.
3. Mildred Freburg Berry, "Abraham Lincoln: His Development in the Skills of the Platform," *History and Criticism of American Public Address* Vol. II, ed. William Norwood Brignance, 828–858 (New York: McGraw-Hill, 1943), 851.

whole state. Flexible wording makes the message applicable at every stop.

Similarly, the preacher who has memorized or developed a manuscript of Sunday's sermon will have much greater difficulty incorporating late-breaking news into the message. By contrast, extemporaneous preachers often buttress the points of their message with local or national news events from Saturday evening or even early Sunday morning. The result is a more relevant and timely message.

AUDIENCE ANALYSIS

Every effective speaker, regardless of delivery style, begins the speech-building process with audience analysis. The analysis that occurs before delivery of the speech may be thought of as extrinsic audience analysis. Because of this analysis, the speaker has a basic understanding of the audience and how it will react to the speech from the first word of the introduction. Delivery is enhanced and communication is more effective because the speaker understands the audience.

Speakers often have another opportunity for audience analysis. In the midst of the speech, audience members provide nonverbal feedback to the speaker that some part of the speech either has or has not been communicated effectively. The speaker who reads these nonverbal cues and adjusts to them has improved delivery by means of *intrinsic audience analysis*.

INTRINSIC AUDIENCE ANALYSIS
A process performed in the midst of delivery in which a speaker evaluates whether or not the speech is being understood by the audience.

Zach delivered a classroom speech in an extemporaneous fashion. At one point in the speech, he noted several audience members with furrowed brows and quizzical looks. Zach realized that he needed to make the point clearer. He reiterated the point by choosing different words and saying the same thing in a different way.

If Zach had used a manuscript, he probably wouldn't have noticed the audience feedback because his eye focus would have been on the manuscript rather than the audience. If Zach had memorized his speech, the best he could have hoped for would be to finish the recitation without losing his place. A speaker using memorized delivery will sometimes encounter audience feedback that forces him to lose his train of thought and stumble over his words. Only the extemporaneous speaker has the public speaking luxury of ongoing adjustment to audience feedback.

Not every incident of intrinsic audience analysis is in response to negative audience feedback. Sometimes a speaker will notice the nodding of heads or audience members leaning forward in their seats. It sends the signal that a particular point is being well received. In that case, the speaker may want to move on or acknowledge the positive feedback as a way of building on audience rapport. Once again, it's only the extemporaneous speaker who can implement the benefits of intrinsic audience analysis.

ONGOING ADJUSTMENT

Sometimes speakers must deal with unexpected events that occur during the course of the speech. Such a moment occurred for Adlai Stevenson. Stevenson is best known as the thirty-third governor of Illinois, and as a United States ambassador to the United Nations from 1961–1965. In addition, he made runs at the White House on the Democratic ticket in 1952 and 1956. During one of those unsuccessful campaigns, the wind blew away several pages of Stevenson's manuscript speech during an open-air rally. Stevenson reportedly looked up at the audience and noted "that's one for you." He then continued reading from the balance of his text.

In 1890, a similar disruption occurred during the campaign for women's suffrage in South Dakota. Susan B. Anthony was addressing a crowd that included a man who was obviously intoxicated. The drunk man interrupted her speech several times before the crowd called for his removal. "No," Anthony said, "he is a product of man's government, and I want you to see what sort you make."[6]

Alex served a small church as student pastor in addition to being a full-time university student. One Sunday morning Alex began his message with a series of rhetorical questions. A little boy unexpectedly shouted out an answer to one of Alex's questions. The congregation erupted in laughter. After the laughter died down, Alex thanked the young parishioner for his response and then built on it to make the first point of his message.

RHETORICAL QUESTION
Question asked by a speaker that is designed for the audience members to answer mentally rather than aloud.

These examples point to the fact that from time to time, all speakers must deal with unexpected events during the course of a speech. Extemporaneous speakers have the best opportunity to make effective adjustments.

With so many advantages to the extemporaneous style of delivery, one might question why all speeches are not carefully prepared and then delivered with few, if any, notes. The answer lies in the fact that extemporaneous speakers face challenges that some are not willing or not able to overcome. These challenges, and overcoming them effectively, are the subject of the next section.

HENRY WARD BEECHER

One of the most prominent preachers of the late 19th century was Henry Ward Beecher. Born in Connecticut in 1813, he was educated at Amherst College and Lane Theological Seminary. While he held pastorates at Lawrenceburg and Indianapolis, Indiana, his most influential sermons were preached at the Plymouth Church in Brooklyn, New York, where he served from 1847 until 1887.

Today, Beecher is remembered for his lectures, newspaper articles, and twenty-four books. His audiences, however, appreciated him for his extemporaneous delivery skills. Lionel Crocker notes that Beecher's outlines contained only the boundaries of his thoughts. The precise wording grew out of his mental interactions with the people before him. Of his own preaching style Beecher declared,

> I know what I am going to aim at, but, of course, I don't get down to anything specific. I brood it, and ponder it, and dream over it, and pick up information about one point or another but if I ever think I see the plan opening up to me I don't dare to look at it or put it down on paper. If once I write a thing out, it is almost impossible for me to kindle to it again. I never dare nowadays, to write out a sermon during the week; that is sure to kill it. I have to think around and about it and get generally ready, and fuse it when the time comes.[1]

When new buildings were constructed under his leadership, he assisted architects in building a speaker's platform that jutted into the audience instead of the more traditional pulpits of the day. He always wanted to speak with the people.

NOTES

1. Lyman Abbott and S. B. Halliday, *Henry Ward Beecher* (Hartford: American Publishing Co., 1988), 130 as cited in Lionel Crocker, "Henry Ward Beecher," *History and Criticism of American Public Address*, Vol. II, ed. William Norwood Brignance, 265–293 (New York: McGraw-Hill) 1943.

2

CHALLENGES TO EXTEMPORANEOUS DELIVERY

Public speaking experts agree that, as with any worthwhile endeavor, there are challenges to effective extemporaneous speaking. The best extemporaneous speakers recognize and respond to these challenges. The nine greatest challenges to extemporaneous speaking include:

- Anxiety
- Time management
- Distracting mannerisms
- Vocalized pauses
- Repeated phrases
- Idea clarity
- Audience feedback
- Overdramatization
- Alternative style

ANXIETY CHALLENGE

In an editorial entitled "Speaking in Public: No Scarier than Flying," Kevin Cowherd addresses the fear of public address. His satirical conclusion asks, "What is the worst that can happen? Your mind goes blank and, terror stricken, you lapse into a catatonic trance? The audience begins hooting and laughing at you? Startled from the trance by a tomato landing on your forehead, you flee the lectern in tears, only to rush home and lock yourself in a dark room for six months? Sure, I guess all that could happen. Then again, it might not. You could be one of the lucky ones."[1]

As Cowherd's satire indicates, the worst-case scenario seldom becomes a reality. Yet one of the greatest challenges to extemporaneous speaking is dealing with the universal anxiety associated with public speaking. This anxiety often results in the speaker making distracting movements that are caused by *working off* an excess of adrenaline. Distracting movements may include shuffling the feet, rocking from side to side, or drumming fingers on the lectern. After viewing her first speech, Angela said that the whole experience left her feeling seasick. From the first word of the introduction to the last word of the conclusion, she moved from one foot to another in a repetitive rocking motion.

While some speakers tend to rock back and forth, others find that the adrenaline freezes them in place. They may clutch the lectern in a white-knuckled grasp or hold their head and body rigid. The adrenaline has a freezing effect on them. It's nearly impossible to predict what kind of impact adrenaline will have on a particular speaker.

That's one reason why everyone must have personal experience at speaking extemporaneously. Experienced extemporaneous speakers have numerous occasions to witness the impact of adrenaline in their particular situation. They either practice away the distracting mannerisms, or plan for meaningful gestures in order to properly manage the anxiety. In addition, experienced extemporaneous speakers focus on three keys to control anxiety.

Embrace Creative Tension. These speakers recognize that the goal is not to avoid anxiety, but to use the anxiety-produced adrenaline in a positive way. Adrenaline can actually produce a more high energy and polished performance.

Start with a Pause. Even before the first word of the speech, experienced speakers take a deep breath (not a gasp), plant their feet firmly, and establish eye contact with their audience. These actions give them the feeling of being in charge and lead to a more polished performance.

Practice Prior to Delivery. Much of what speakers refer to as public speaking anxiety is actually fear of the unknown. Not adequately practicing the speech prior to delivery enhances the fear. Prepared extemporaneous speakers have rehearsed the speech several times prior to delivery. Practice gives them reason to believe that the end result of the speaking assignment will be positive. They have minimized the unknown element because they have prepared.

TIME MANAGEMENT CHALLENGE

Beginning extemporaneous speakers often practice their speech with a particular assigned time frame in mind. But after the actual delivery, they're amazed to hear that the time is significantly less than what they practiced. Anxiety causes them to speak faster in front of the audience.

Jay worked hard on the development of his first sermon after he became the pastor of a small-town church. Each practice session lasted between twenty and twenty-five minutes, and he was pleased with the outline and idea development. After he finished the Sunday morning sermon, however, Jay noticed several parishioners looking at their watches in surprise. Jay's sermon had lasted only twelve minutes.

Occasionally, a beginning extemporaneous speaker will slow down and deliver a long speech because of adrenaline. More typically, however, the too-long speech can be attributed to lack of preparation and practice.

Time management is a problem that can be solved by consciously practicing slower delivery. A speaker who experiences a hurried delivery can learn to anticipate the problem and plan more speech content in order to compensate. By the third week in his pastorate, Jay found that he was delivering normal-length sermons. He was also amazed at the amount of content he could introduce in that time frame.

DISTRACTING MANNERISMS CHALLENGE

As previously noted, the anxiety of giving a speech sometimes creates distracting mannerisms that a speaker must work to overcome. In other cases, distractions are natural to the speaker and are not the product of anxiety at all. These must also be minimized in order to maximize the impact of the extemporaneous delivery. Examples of such distracting behaviors follow.

Greg's glasses did not fit properly. As a result they were constantly sliding down his nose. Greg corrected the problem by pushing the glasses up repeatedly during the delivery of his speech. A natural mannerism for Greg became a distraction for his audience.

Sam had something of a perspiration problem. During his sermon in homiletics class, he repeatedly wiped his brow with his handkerchief. The mannerism created a distraction for Sam's audience.

Paula was one of the few married students in her public speaking class. She had developed the habit of spinning her wedding ring on her finger with the thumb of her left hand. The mannerism became a major distraction to her audience.

In each of these cases, the speakers discovered the distracting mannerism when they watched their speech on videotape. Then they set out to develop a systematic program for eliminating the distraction.

Eliminating distracting mannerisms when practicing your speech will, at times, prove adequate. In most cases, however, the mannerism must be minimized in non-speaking situations before it can be eliminated at the podium or lectern.

ROBERT KENNEDY

Robert "Bobby" Kennedy, younger brother of President John F. Kennedy, was born on November 20, 1925, in Brookline, Massachusetts. He was the United States Attorney General from 1961 until 1964. He broke with the Johnson administration over the War in Vietnam and became a senator from New York. Kennedy was best known for his strong support of civil rights legislation. He campaigned for the Democratic nomination for president in 1968. Minutes after accepting victory in the California primary in June 1968, he was killed by a gunman.

Just a few months earlier, on April 4 of that same year, Kennedy was scheduled to address an evening rally in Indianapolis, Indiana. After his plane landed, police advised him of the assassination of Dr. Martin Luther King, Jr. earlier that same day in Memphis. Fearing violence from the largely African American crowd, police recommended canceling the appearance. Instead, Kennedy spent only a few minutes in preparation before delivering an extemporaneous speech of about six minutes at the airport. While a case could be made that the speech is impromptu, the largely unused notes in Kennedy's right hand seem to indicate that he did have an outline of his main points and delivered those points extemporaneously.

In the speech, Kennedy announced the death of King and urged the audience to search for understanding, compassion, and love. Kennedy advised, "We have to make an effort in the United States, we have to make an effort to understand, to get beyond these rather difficult times." He ended the speech by urging audience members to return home and pray for the Kings and for the nation.

The speech may be viewed in its entirety at AmericanRhetoric.com.

VOCALIZED PAUSE CHALLENGE

Twenty-first-century Americans live in constant noise. Horns honk. Phones ring. Kids scream. Radios blare. Neighbors argue. Televisions play. Jets roar. The result is a noisy world in which many Americans have developed a low tolerance for silence.

This low tolerance is sharply intensified when standing before an audience. The speaker feels as if the entire assembly expects her to eliminate the unusual and intolerable silence. A speaker may report that a mere two-second pause feels like a full minute of sheer agony. Speakers thus comply with their assumed responsibility for such unnatural silence by means of a *vocalized pause*.

A vocalized pause is a meaningless or improperly used sound that fills the silence at a place in the speech where brief quiet is all that is really needed. Vocalized pauses often occur at the end of a sentence where the period allows a moment for breathing. In fact, a breath is what is best. Instead, many extemporaneous speakers use the guttural *uh* or *um* in order to fill the silence.

VOCALIZED PAUSE
The sound occurring when a speaker fills the necessary pause with words or sounds that are not necessary to the speech. *Um* is the most common vocalized pause.

Uh or *um* have no real meaning and add nothing positive to the speech. Its only purpose is to get the speaker off the hook by filling the silence. These gutturals also serve to distract the audience, and often cause audience members to evaluate the speaker more negatively.

Sometimes the vocalized pause is a misused word rather than a non-word guttural. These misused words often lose their original meaning and spread throughout the speech in a distracting manner.

The word *like* is one of the most interesting of the vocalized pauses. The word has gained popularity in conversation as a vocalized pause. The increased usage follows many speakers to the lectern. Properly used, *like* is a term that compares two subjects or items. The term expresses similarity.

For example, "A class in Old Testament Survey is like one in New Testament Survey in many respects." Here the word *like* is used correctly since it compares the similarities in the two classes.

A second sentence demonstrates the same word as a vocalized pause. "Like I really enjoy the Old Testament class because it's like my easiest class." Here the word is used incorrectly—as a vocalized pause. If *like* were eliminated from this sentence entirely the meaning would become clearer. "I really enjoy the Old Testament class because it's my easiest class."

Other examples of misused vocalized pauses include:

- Okay?
- You know what I mean?
- See?
- And so on
- Listen
- Or whatever
- Like I said before
- My next point is
- Et cetera
- Y'know?

The best extemporaneous speakers seek to eliminate the vocalized pauses from their speech by minimizing them in everyday conversation. Speakers may flag certain words in their minds. They force themselves to notice when those words come up in conversations. Then it's a simple matter to substitute more appropriate words or simply breathe and tolerate the silence.

Effective extemporaneous speakers remember that silence is not the enemy. Instead of being embarrassed by a few seconds of silence, they note that the audience offers them undivided attention during these times. These speakers learn to use the silence to their advantage.

REPEATED PHRASE CHALLENGE

The *repeated phrase* is another challenge that extemporaneous speakers frequently face. Repeated phrases may be used correctly, but too frequently. Since the precise words of the speech are determined at the point of delivery, it is possible for the speaker to use the same words or phrases over and over again. This may become distracting to audience members.

Extemporaneous speakers often overcome this challenge through repeated practice of the speech. With each practice session, they force themselves to use slightly different words and phrases in order to express the same ideas. When the speech is finally delivered before a live audience, the speaker has an extensive lexicon of possible terms from which to choose.

A long-term approach to meeting the repeated phrase challenge is to improve one's vocabulary. Speakers who read a lot gain greater exposure to words and language structure. In addition, these speakers often develop personal programs to learn new words on a regular basis. They recognize that the more words they have at their disposal, the less likely they will be to overuse one word or phrase.

IDEA CLARITY CHALLENGE

Another challenge to the extemporaneous speaker is maintaining *idea clarity*. Ironically, this is often the greatest challenge for those who find speaking in front of an audience relatively easy. These speakers tend to ramble from one thought to another in the delivery of their speech.

When Brittany delivered a speech to inform others about her recent experience on a Caribbean cruise, she fell prey to the idea clarity challenge. Brittany had recently returned from the cruise and was excited to tell others about her experience. She rambled about the good entertainment, the good food, the best way to choose a cruise line, which type of room to select, what to take along, and problems to avoid. By the end of the speech, Brittany had shared everything she knew about cruises. But she also left the audience exhausted from trying to keep up with her, and she had gone over her allotted time.

Speakers who struggle with the idea clarity challenge will do well to remember that extemporaneous speeches need a clear outline. Only the precise words for developing that outline are chosen on the spur of the moment. Some speakers avoid rambling by memorizing the key points they intend to cover. Others use a presentation outline to highlight the points. Such an outline can usually be accomplished on one three-by-five card. The three or four words that represent the main points of the speech are sufficient for such an outline.

AUDIENCE FEEDBACK CHALLENGE

Since extemporaneous speakers are developing the precise language of the speech during the actual delivery, they are very dependent upon the feedback of audience members. A nod of the head or a knowing smile lets the speaker know that the point is understood and acknowledged. By contrast, a wrinkled brow or other quizzical look communicates to the speaker that the point is not clear.

This dependence upon audience feedback provides a great opportunity for the speaker to be successful. At the same time, it may cause the speaker some difficulty. That's because not all audience members are expressive. Some may understand thoroughly but their lack of expression makes it impossible for the speaker to know it. Because of this, those who do communicate nonverbally through facial expressions will often become the sole focus of the extemporaneous speaker.

JOHN WESLEY

Adherents to the theology and ecclesiology of John Wesley often point to May 24, 1738, as the turning point in his life and ministry. On that day, Wesley visited Aldersgate Street Church and heard a reading from Luther's preface to the *Commentary on the Epistle to the Romans*. He later noted in his journal, "I felt my heart strangely warmed. I felt I did trust in Christ, Christ alone for salvation; and an assurance was given me that he had taken away my sins, even mine and saved me from the law of sin and death."[1]

But perhaps the date April 2, 1739, also deserves mention for the most significant date in the life of the founder of the Methodist movement. On that date, Wesley reluctantly agreed to preach outside the confines of the church. He wrote of the change, "At four in the afternoon I submitted to be more vile and proclaimed in the highways the glad tidings of salvation."[2]

Wesley thus noted his reluctant decision to begin *field preaching*—his term for preaching out of doors. The concept was revolutionary in 18th century England, and unacceptable to the formal Church of England.

The attempt to relate to the common hearer not only moved Wesley out of doors, but forced him to use language that was "plain, proper and clear." He later urged the preachers under his authority to do the same.

Over the course of nearly fifty years, he traveled between four and five thousand miles annually, and preached over forty thousand sermons. As many as ten thousand people would turn out just to hear him preach. Wesley helped to ignite the fires of revival that burned across England and the New World. The impact of John Wesley's spiritual awakening is still felt today.

NOTES

1. *The Works of John Wesley,* 3rd ed., Vol. 1 (repr., Grand Rapids: Baker, 1978) 103.
2. Ibid., 185.

When Paul preached his first sermon in his home church, he noticed that Mrs. Wright was nodding and smiling her appreciation for Paul's message. Paul took these gestures as indication that he was communicating effectively with the congregation. A conversation after the service caused Paul to realize that Mrs. Wright was extremely proud of him since she had taught him in Sunday school during his elementary years. Her expressions would have been positive even if Paul's message was totally unintelligible.

Other speakers have discovered that their eye contact is drawn to the most expressive people to the exclusion of the rest of the audience. The best extemporaneous speakers force themselves to maintain eye contact with a large segment of the audience, including those who provide no special feedback.

OVERDRAMATIZATION CHALLENGE

There is a great deal of similarity between the performance of an actor and the performance of a speaker. Both communicate with an audience and both must practice to maximize that performance.

On the other hand, there are some significant differences between the two. An actor assumes the role of the character being portrayed, while the best speakers perform by simply being themselves. Because audiences prefer a heightened conversation style of delivery, speakers should avoid being stiff and mechanical. But they should also avoid going to the extreme of acting a part. Practicing the speech over and over so that the speaker can comfortably and confidently communicate the main points is an important key to successful speaking.

THE ALTERNATIVE STYLE CHALLENGE

For certain speakers, settings, or speeches, an alternative to extemporaneous speaking may be appropriate. But all too frequently, beginning speakers face one or more of the challenges to extemporaneous speaking and fall prey to the ultimate challenge of selecting an alternative delivery style because it appears easier. The primary alternatives to extemporaneous delivery are impromptu delivery, manuscript delivery, and memorized delivery. Each style has a legitimate time and place in public speaking, but none are adequate substitutes for effective extemporaneous delivery.

In popular language, *extemporaneous* is often used synonymously with *impromptu*. Technically, however, the terms have very different meanings. An impromptu speech is one that is delivered with only a few seconds of preparation. For example, business people may use impromptu speech when called upon in a meeting to respond to a proposal. Students may use impromptu speech when a faculty member asks a question. Most people have given hundreds of impromptu speeches before they ever enroll in a public speaking class.

- A Sunday school teacher says, "Please introduce your guest."
- A friend asks during an informal gathering in the dorm, "Which faculty member do you recommend for New Testament Survey?"
- A manager asks, "Could you explain your report to our committee?"

An appropriate response in each of these scenarios requires a brief impromptu speech. Some students get so proficient at giving impromptu speeches that they attempt to use that delivery style when their public speaking instructor assigns a speech that is to be more carefully prepared. Substituting impromptu delivery for extemporaneous is a poor strategy that leads to less than maximum outcomes.

Similarly, the manuscript style of speaking is sometimes necessary and appropriate. But not when the circumstances call for extemporaneous. When the president of the United States addresses a joint session of Congress, the audience may include several million television viewers from around the world. Press analysts review the speech before and after the delivery, looking at every word for hidden or implied meaning. Such situations call for a carefully worded and rehearsed manuscript speech. In situations where precise wording or technical language is required, a manuscript delivery is perhaps preferable to extemporaneous. On these occasions, several manuscript delivery tips will aid the speaker.

- Type the manuscript double or triple space for ease in reading. It helps to maintain the appearance of eye contact.
- Type on only one side of the paper in order to avoid lost places or flipping pages during the reading of the speech.
- Adjust the podium to a proper reading height in order to maximize the appearance of eye contact.
- Highlight the manuscript to indicate proper places to pause and gesture.
- Use additional highlighting to indicate the proper places to add voice inflections and changes in pitch, rate, and volume.
- While reading the manuscript, slide completed pages to the side rather than raising or flipping them.

Some speakers have used these tips, along with a great deal of practice, and have become very effective at delivering manuscript speeches. Experience indicates, however, that for every individual that achieves an effective manuscript style, there are several others who would have benefited from the extra effort required to deliver extemporaneously.

Another alternative to extemporaneous speaking is delivering the speech from memory. In the earliest days of oratory, it was common for speakers to demonstrate their skill by memorizing and delivering very long speeches. Those who give the same speech repeatedly today, such as political candidates on the stump or motivational speakers on the lecture circuit, may use a memorized delivery. Others avoid memorized delivery since the payoff for the additional work is typically just a stiff, formal style of delivery. Forgetting portions of the speech and thus destroying the delivery is another reason why speakers avoid this style.

Occasionally a beginning public speaking student will memorize a classroom speech believing that memorization will yield reduced anxiety. In fact the opposite is usually the result. The speaker may end up staring at the floor or ceiling whispering the previous line repeatedly in a usually futile effort to remember. Generally entire speeches should not be memorized unless the speaking assignment is very brief, such as the speech required for a toast at a wedding or the introduction of a featured speaker. Most other times, a speaker does well to effectively deliver the speech or sermon in an extemporaneous manner.

When she wrote about alternative methods of delivery, one public speaking expert noted, "The goal of manuscript speaking is to sound as if you are engaged in direct conversation."[2] In other words, even when circumstances force a speaker to use an alternative delivery style, the goal is to *appear* extemporaneous. But the best speakers avoid settling for just the appearance of extemporaneous speaking and simply speak extemporaneously.

The extra effort needed to overcome the challenges to extemporaneous delivery pays enormous dividends in the form of excellent results. But these results don't just happen. They come about through careful preparation. That is why the next two sections focus on preparing and delivering an effective extemporaneous speech.

GEORGE WHITEFIELD

One of the best-known evangelists of the First Great Awakening was George Whitefield. He was born in Gloucester, England, in December of 1714, to a widow who was the innkeeper in that city. He worked his way through the Crypt School and later the Pembroke College in Oxford. It was noted that early in his life, he had a great talent and flare for the dramatic and was encouraged to pursue a career in theatre.

Instead, Whitefield journeyed to America in 1738, where he became the priest of the Church of England at Savannah, Georgia. There he continued the open air preaching that he had first begun in Bristol. This speaking style and location greatly appealed to the Americans. It's noted that the influential Benjamin Franklin once heard Whitefield preach in Philadelphia and was greatly appreciative of the power of the pulpit master's oratory.

Whitefield was a strong advocate and effective example of extemporaneous preaching. His preaching was known for its drama and fervor. Clarence Macartney notes that Whitefield was attacked by professors at Harvard for preaching without notes. It was their belief that an argument could not be handled convincingly without the development of a manuscript. They accused Whitefield of avoiding the hard work of preaching by his extemporaneous style.

Whitefield responded, "Let no one choose this method because he thinks thus to deliver himself from the bondage of pen or memory. By no means! Preaching without notes is by all odds the hardest way, both as to preparation and delivery."[1]

In spite of the challenges associated with it, Whitefield chose the extemporaneous way because he discovered the power of such effective oratory.

NOTES

1. Clarence Edward Macartney. *Preaching Without Notes* (New York: Abingdon, 1946), 145.

3

PREPARING AN EXTEMPORANEOUS SPEECH

In an Introduction to Public Speaking class, one student argued that he should not have to take such a course. "What's to learn?" he asked. "I already know how to talk." Many others who have taken similar courses have used the same logic to justify not preparing for a speech.

By contrast Ralph L. Lewis, professor of preaching at Asbury Theological Seminary, once declared that the best speakers spend an hour of preparation for every minute of public address. "That's twenty hours of preparation for a twenty-minute sermon," he reminded his homiletics students.

The truth lies somewhere between these two extremes. No one ever delivered their most effective extemporaneous speech without some preparation. Yet, most people don't have an hour per minute to devote to preparation. The secret to success lies not in spending enormous amounts of time in preparation, but in using the preparation time wisely and effectively. To that end this section focuses on eight steps in the speech preparation process.

STEP 1: SELECT A TOPIC AND GENERAL PURPOSE

The first step in the development of an effective extemporaneous speech usually happens without much forethought or planning. That is the selection of a general purpose and topic for the speech. Sometimes this selection is done for the speaker. When a contact person for a group calls to issue an invitation to speak, he or she may assign a specific theme, or at the very least suggest a general topic area.

In the absence of a particular assignment, the speaker will need to decide the general purpose of the speech. This will include whether the speech is to inform, persuade, edify, or celebrate. In addition, the speaker would do well to select a preliminary general topic.

STEP 2: EVALUATE THE SPEAKING SITUATION

Before the first word is spoken—even before the first word is planned—the speaker must engage in the data collection process known as audience analysis. Audience analysis takes place when the speaker learns as much as possible about the audience and setting for the upcoming speech.

The speaker will want to gather demographic information about the audience. Demographics include such information as the age, ethnicity, gender, and education of audience members. This demographic audience analysis will yield data that will help the speaker determine the interests and background of audience members.

DEMOGRAPHIC AUDIENCE ANALYSIS Audience analysis that focuses on factors such as the age, gender, education level, or ethnicity of audience members.

The speaker will also want to determine the audience's belief system and attitude about the topic for the speech. This information is sometimes referred to as psychological audience analysis. Such data collection may include

PSYCHOLOGICAL AUDIENCE ANALYSIS Audience analysis that focuses on audience members' predisposition to the topic of the speech.

the audience's previous exposure to the topic. What have they already decided? How much education do they have on the topic? What are their preconceptions?

Complete audience analysis will also include analyzing the size of the audience and the physical surroundings in which the speech will be given. This vital information is known as *situational audience analysis*. The time of day for which the speech is scheduled, the temperature of the room, and the availability of technological support for the speech are all important parts of a complete situational analysis.

Collecting all of this data can be a daunting task. But there are several sources of information available to the speaker. One of the most obvious collection points is the contact person of the group arranging the speech. The well-prepared speaker will ask a number of questions about the event, audience, group makeup and size, and general expectations. Experienced speakers make sure they have the phone number or e-mail address of the contact person in the event that follow-up questions become necessary.

SITUATIONAL AUDIENCE ANALYSIS Audience analysis that focuses on the situational factors surrounding the speech. Such factors might include audience size, time of day, or room size in which the speech is delivered.

In addition to the contact person, speakers often gain the information they need through interviews and surveys. These should also focus on the group members that will make up the audience. Usually such data collection is representative of the group rather than involving every member of the audience. In smaller groups, on the other hand, the entire audience is sometimes surveyed. When Joel did a persuasive speech on capital punishment for his public speaking class, he surveyed the class in order to determine their attitudes on the subject. Then he knew what persuasive agenda was most likely to be accomplished and what was most needed by the audience.

INTELLECTUAL AUDIENCE ANALYSIS
Audience analysis data that is collected by the speaker by simply contemplating the audience and its makeup.

Sometimes the speaker can gather adequate data by simply contemplating the audience makeup and inferring their attitudes and beliefs about a particular topic. This process is called *intellectual audience analysis*. The speaker will need to exercise extreme caution not to engage in stereotyping during this form of analysis.

STEP 3: CREATE A SPECIFIC PURPOSE

A *specific purpose statement* is a one-sentence statement indicating what the speaker hopes to accomplish in the speech. The specific purpose statement should be written as a complete sentence, should declare what the speaker wants to impart to the audience, and should use clear and precise language.

SPECIFIC PURPOSE STATEMENT
A one sentence statement indicating what the speaker hopes to accomplish in the speech.

As the development of the speech unfolds, the specific purpose statement becomes the guiding light that illuminates what information is helpful and what is not. Hence the specific purpose statement should be written very early in the speech-building process. The tongue-in-cheek adage, "If you don't know where you're going, you'll get there every time," is very true and relevant in speech building. The well-written, specific purpose statement serves to remind the speaker of the ultimate goal throughout the speech-building process.

APOSTOLIC PREACHERS

The earliest post-resurrection preachers appear to have adopted an extemporaneous style of delivery. While the term and direct evidence do not appear in Scripture "It is difficult, if not impossible to picture . . . Paul reading his sermon to the philosophers on Mars Hill, or Peter unrolling a scroll on the day of Pentecost to read the divine summons to repent and believe."[1]

In the meeting of the Areopagas in Athens, Paul tailors his remarks around an earlier tour of the city and its religious artifacts. "Men of Athens! I see that in every way you are very religious. For as I walked around and looked carefully at your objects of worship, I even found an altar with the inscription: To an unknown God. Now what you worship as something unknown I am going to proclaim to you."[2] The fact that Paul was not tied to a memorized text or manuscript allowed him to fit at least the introduction of his message to the immediate audience.

Similarly, on the day of Pentecost, the coming of the Holy Spirit was not anticipated; thus Peter's sermon responding to the event could not have been memorized or written in manuscript form. As a result Peter was able to mesh his remarks with the events of the day in true extemporaneous style. "Then Peter stood up with the eleven, raised his voice, and addressed the crowd."[3]

NOTES

1. Ralph Lewis, "Preaching With and Without Notes," *Handbook of Contemporary Preaching*, ed. Michael Duduit (Nashville: Broadman, 1992), 409–419.
2. Acts 17:22–23.
3. Acts 2:14.

STEP 4: CREATE A THESIS STATEMENT

The fourth step is to write a *thesis statement*. It grows out of the specific purpose statement. As with any well-written thesis or term paper, the speaker should declare the precise intention of the speech. The thesis statement is usually included in the introduction of the speech. Examples of thesis statements include:

- Today I want to teach you the steps involved in changing a tire: loosen, jack, remove, replace, lower, and tighten.
- In this speech I hope to convince you to reevaluate your views on capital punishment by considering the biblical mandate and the evidence of deterrence.
- In the next few minutes, I intend to help you revitalize your prayer life by praying with the ACTS acronym of adoration, confession, thanksgiving, and supplication.
- This afternoon I will offer to you the three most important reasons why John Artez should be the president of student council, based on his experience, his integrity, and his willingness to listen.

THESIS STATEMENT
A statement indicating precisely what steps the speaker will take to accomplish the purpose of the speech.

Sometimes beginning speakers avoid writing a specific purpose or thesis statement until preliminary research has been accomplished. They argue that they cannot develop them until they know that the information is available on that topic. This practice ignores the advantages available in the modern information age. Today's speech writer has information available at the click of a mouse on virtually every conceivable subject and position. It's advantageous to create the specific purpose and thesis statement of the speech as early as possible. Then the speaker is better able to identify the information that best supports that thesis.

STEP 5: OBTAIN MATERIAL FOR THE SPEECH

Researching a speech is the process of finding the necessary information to develop the points of the speech. The research process will lead the speaker to one (or more) of four sources of information, including experiential sources, printed sources, electronic sources, and speaker-developed sources.

RESEARCH
The process of gathering information for the speech.

Experiential sources include those pieces of information that the speaker already knows, and which support the points of the speech. Usually the speaker will choose a topic of personal interest. In this case, personal experience becomes a great source of speech information. Even when the speaker does not have information available that translates directly to the speech, he or she will know the shortcuts to find the information because of personal experiences.

Printed sources are those sources typically found in a library. Much of the information stored in a library has been converted to electronic form, but some sources remain available only in hard copy. Many researchers suggest a final check of information be done via printed form since the accuracy of printed sources is more easily confirmed. Some of the available printed sources include almanacs, atlases, biographical collections, commentaries, dictionaries, encyclopedias, indexes, journals, magazines, newspapers, quotation collections, and yearbooks.

Electronic sources include altered forms of many of the printed sources. Many electronic sources include collections of information stored electronically. These collections, called *databases*, can save the researcher enormous amounts of time. Search engines are also available to the modern researcher and prove to be tremendous time savers. In spite of the fact that the larger search engines provide access to more than three billion current Web sites,[1] the best engines still explore only a small fraction of the information available on the Web.[2]

Speaker-developed sources are those that the speaker generates through primary research. Interviews and questionnaires are among the most common speaker-developed sources. When the speech is a sermon or Sunday school lesson, the speaker-developed research process involves careful inductive Bible study. This systematic study, designed to unlock the truths of Scripture, is called exegesis. Several authors have addressed the best procedures for gleaning information from Scripture.[3] Utilizing one of these resources carefully will yield tremendous positive results.

STEP 6: PLAN THE BASIC STRUCTURE

Armed with a well-written purpose and thesis statement, and the data collected from research, the extemporaneous speaker is now ready to organize the speech. It usually works best to let the data do the organization itself. At other times speakers create an outline and then fill in the appropriate data under each point and subpoint.

Both Courtney and Zach decided to do their informative speech on golf. They were in separate sections of Dr. Parker's Introduction to Public Speaking class, so he allowed them to use the same thesis statement and work together on researching the speech. They agreed on the statement, "In this speech I will reveal to the audience the location of the six best golf courses in the state of Indiana."

At this point, the similarities between Courtney and Zach's approach ended. Courtney outlined the speech early and decided that it made sense to use a two-part speech. She decided on the two-part outline:

1. Northern Indiana courses
2. Southern Indiana courses

Zach, on the other hand, let the data speak for itself. He noted that four of the six best courses in the state were in the metropolitan Indianapolis area. His two-part outline was:

1. Greater Indianapolis courses
2. Courses outside Indianapolis

While Zach finished this step in the process and moved on to the next step in speech building, Courtney struggled with what latitude should be used to divide the state and make sure the points of her speech were parallel. There are times where it just works better to let the outline come from the research rather than imposing an outline on the data.

Regardless of which approach the speaker uses to plan the basic structure, the process should lead to a preparation outline that clearly demonstrates the main points and appropriate subpoints of the speech. An extemporaneous speaker will not need to write out a manuscript of the speech. Since word choices will be made at the point of formal delivery, the preparation time, which might be used to write out a speech, will be better used on steps seven and eight of the preparation process.

STEP 7: DEVELOP AN INTRODUCTION AND CONCLUSION

Research indicates that people who are exposed to verbal stimuli have a tendency to remember the first and last thing they hear, while recalling later much less of what they heard in between.[4] Some experts believe that the first thing heard is the most powerful, while others indicate that the last thing will be retained longer.[5] Either way, this research, known as *primacy* and *recency*, has clear implications in the area of public speaking. The primacy event (introduction) and the recency event (conclusion) will be the most memorable portions of the speech for audience members. Therefore, the introduction and conclusion should occupy a major portion of the speech preparation time.

Effective introductions should gain the attention of the audience and establish the credibility of the speaker on the topic at

INTRODUCTION
The opening of the speech which is designed to gain the attention of the audience, establish the credibility of the speaker, and reveal the outline of the speech.

hand. An effective introduction also previews the speech for the audience so that they know what to expect as it unfolds. The speaker subtly reveals the thesis statement of the speech in the introduction. While introductions are important, they must accomplish these key purposes in a short amount of time. In fact, speech experts suggest that the introduction should occupy only 10 to 15 percent of the total speech.[6]

Conclusions, on the other hand, are the last chance a speaker has to make a favorable impression on the audience. They should reinforce the thesis and summarize the main points of the speech. The best conclusions seem to refer back to the introduction of the speech thus tying the whole speech together as a package. An illustration or quotation is often used in the conclusion in order to make the speech memorable. As with the introduction, the conclusion should be a brief portion of the speech. The best conclusions occupy only 5 to 10 percent of the total speech.[7]

CONCLUSION
The ending of the speech should reinforce the thesis and summarize the main points of the speech.

Extemporaneous speakers differ as to the best method of delivering the introduction and conclusion. Some argue that these portions of the speech are so vital to the total presentation that they should be memorized or written in manuscript form. It seems logical, however, to remain consistent in the style and delivery. The best delivery style for the introduction and conclusion is still the extemporaneous style.

STEP 8: REHEARSE

Imagine being part of a theatrical performance where one of the performers does not rehearse with the other actors. Even if that actor reads the play carefully and memorizes the lines meticulously, one can hardly expect a stellar performance. Rehearsal is a vital part of the preparation. Rehearsal is also essential to effective delivery in extemporaneous speaking.

Effective extemporaneous speakers practice their speech repeatedly before delivering it to the intended audience. Some maintain that practicing before a mirror helps them to perfect the nonverbal elements of the performance. Others gather a small audience of friends or colleagues to critique the speech and offer suggestions for improvement. Some tape themselves practicing the speech to help them see where adjustments are needed. In a study where participants were asked to identify their level of willingness to speak publicly, it was discovered that watching a videotape of the performance was one of the few activities that increased that willingness.[8]

Regardless of the procedure used for rehearsal sessions, the importance of practice before delivery cannot be overemphasized. The speaker must carefully rehearse in order to effectively deliver the speech and leave the lectern to thunderous applause. This moment of delivery is the focus of the final section.

JESUS OF NAZARETH

It's impossible to know for sure what style of preaching Jesus used during his earthly ministry. There is some evidence, however, that he may have tended toward an extemporaneous delivery.

Luke records the premier sermon of Jesus in the fourth chapter of his gospel. After reading a text from the prophet Isaiah, Jesus "rolled up the scroll, gave it back to the attendant and sat down. The eyes of everyone in the synagogue were fastened on him, and he began by saying to them, 'Today this scripture is fulfilled in your hearing.'"[1]

It's impossible to imagine Jesus reading that introduction from a manuscript. Surely at least this portion of the message was extemporaneous. The reaction to the message is interesting. "All spoke well of him and were amazed at the gracious words that came from his lips."[2]

Along the Sea of Galilee, Jesus preached the comprehensive and compelling sermon that became known as the Sermon on the Mount. In order to argue that he used a manuscript or even extensive notes, one must concede that his attention was drawn from what might have been written, to the environment in which he spoke. "Look at the birds of the air, they do not sow or reap or store away in barns, and yet your heavenly Father feeds them."[3] "See how the lilies of the field grow. They do not labor or spin. Yet I tell you that not even Solomon in all his splendor was not dressed like one of these."[4] Once again "when Jesus had finished saying these things the crowds were amazed . . ."[5]

NOTES

1. Luke 4:20–21.
2. Luke 4:22.
3. Matthew 6:26.
4. Matthew 6:28–29.
5. Matthew 7:28.

4

DELIVERING AN EXTEMPORANEOUS SPEECH

People who have been completely captivated by a speaker and say to themselves, "I wish I could hold an audience's attention like that," were probably listening to an extemporaneous speaker. Extemporaneous speaking affords the speaker more opportunities to engage the audience than any other method of delivery. This section focuses on the opportunities for enhanced delivery that extemporaneous speaking provides.

A well-prepared speaker who is not tied to a manuscript can more effectively capture and engage an audience by devoting more energy and attention to the tools of delivery. These tools allow a speaker to grab and hold an audience. The three primary tools available are body, voice, and words.

The relative importance of each of these varies by speaking situation. Differing views also exist among speech experts on the relative value of each. But there is complete agreement in that the effective employment of these tools results in an audience that enjoys, rather than endures, a speech.

BODY

The body of the speaker is used as an important tool in extemporaneous speaking. Three major aspects of this tool are appearance, movement, and facial expression.

Appearance is a key factor in the credibility assigned to a speaker by an audience. Audience members listen more carefully and assign greater credibility to a speaker that they deem to be attractive.[1] General guidelines for a public speaker's appearance can be found in almost any primary text in public speaking. The present focus is upon elements that relate specifically to extemporaneous speaking.

Good posture communicates a level of confidence that invites the audience to be comfortable with a speaker and find that speaker credible. Beginning speakers often mistake rigidity for standing with confidence. Standing like an overstuffed scarecrow will not inspire audiences. Those who effectively inspire confidence appear natural. But what is natural?

While there is no definitive answer to that question, a working answer might be that natural posture allows the speaker to feel comfortable without appearing awkward to the audience. Both elements of this definition are significant.

For example, Jim used a posture that he found comfortable. His hands hung in front of him with one hand on top of the other in what is called a fig leaf stance. Jim was very comfortable with this because he felt secure, but this position looked awkward to the audience. Jim's posture therefore, would not be considered natural.

By contrast, the best extemporaneous speakers recognize the speaker's body as a visual aid. Leaving any visual aid in front of an audience too long creates a natural loss of interest. Since the speaker is going to be in front of the audience for an extended period of time, he or she must find a way to maintain audience interest. Pointing to the head when talking about thoughts, or to the heart when talking about feelings, is an effective use of the body as a visual aid. Speakers can create variety in the use of the body as a visual aid by incorporating movement.

Movement can be put in two major categories. One is gestures—or the use of hands, arms, and the upper body. The second is moving the entire body in the space that is available.

The extemporaneous speaker can communicate a great deal of information through the use of gesture. There are two types of gestures typically used by the extemporaneous speaker. There are gestures used for illustration and gestures used for emphasis.

Gestures used for illustration give visual reinforcement to the words being spoken. When Tracy was making reference to the biblical account of David and Goliath, he said, "David took five stones." He held up five fingers to illustrate the five stones. Later, when talking about how David swung the stone in the sling around and around, Tracy raised one arm above his head and swung it in a circular motion. Later in the speech, Tracy talked about the courage David felt in his heart. Tracy tapped himself on the chest. When Tracy described how Goliath began to wobble before he fell, he swayed his upper body back and forth. All of these were gestures for illustration.

Gestures are also used to emphasize, draw attention to, or dramatize some word or phrase within a speech. When Tracy talked about David feeling the power of God upon him as he slung the stone, he clenched both fists and crossed his arms in front of him. He held his hands as if he were someone trying to get another to stop as he described David pausing to reflect as he chose the stones.

Extemporaneous speaking allows the speaker the freedom to integrate gestures into the delivery of the speech. When a speaker uses a gesture and sees a quizzical look on the faces of several audience members, he can adjust and try another gesture in an attempt to help them better understand. Speaking from a manuscript eliminates the opportunity to adjust and complete the feedback loop.

In addition to gestures, general body movements play an important role in extemporaneous speaking. A key aspect of this is the use of the space available to the speaker. Because extemporaneous speakers are not bound by a script, they can move around freely and utilize the space around them. But speakers should not move just to move. Every movement should have purpose and meaning. The movements of a speaker who paces back and forth like a caged tiger creates distraction and causes the audience to lose interest. On the other hand, if that same speaker moves slowly toward a member of the audience like a tiger stalking prey in a natural enclosure, the audience's interest is held throughout the movement—even if it takes an extended period of time. Such a movement is enhanced if it also illustrates the point the speaker is making at the moment.

Extemporaneous speakers should attempt to make use of the full stage. While it may not always be a stage that the speaker works from, it's important to learn to use the area available much as an actor would use the space of a stage. If Seth is trying to illustrate the amount of concrete in the Hoover Dam by describing it as enough concrete to make a two lane highway from San Francisco to New York, he might move to the wall to his right and touch it with his hand and say, "San Francisco." Then he can move to the wall on his left and say, "New York." He can even pause at various points on the platform to approximate the locations of other major cities and say, "not to Denver, not to Indianapolis, but all the way to New York." In addition to involving the audience and keeping their interest, Seth has given them a great visual reference for just how much concrete is in the dam.

Another element of movement that extemporaneous speakers should take advantage of is the use of multiple levels. This is another way to keep the audience engaged and to illustrate key portions of the speech. If Heather is telling the story of Jack and the Beanstalk, she might step up onto a chair to play the part of the giant. When she takes the part of Jack she could crouch down or perhaps get on her knees. This use of levels is one of the options available to the extemporaneous speaker.

Yet another aspect of movement involves moving into the audience. Extemporaneous speaking allows the speaker to engage an audience this way. Moving into the audience allows the speaker to engage them by being among them. It raises the audience's energy level by creating some uncertainty. It also involves the audience physically and requires them to shift their positions if they want to maintain visual contact with the speaker.

Another vital arrow in the quiver of the extemporaneous speaker is facial expression. One student referred to the facial expressions of Dr. Martin Luther King, Jr. in his "I have a dream" speech as meaningless. "In such a large crowd," he explained, "only those in the first few rows of people could even see his face." But facial expression is even important to audience members that can not see the speaker's face because the face primes the voice.

An exercise with a classmate serves to illustrate. One student looks at another and shares a phrase used on a regular basis as if it were being shared with a friend. Then the same student shares the same phrase without any facial expression. No cheating on this one. The participant's face must be completely expressionless. When the facial expression is gone, so is the vocal expression.

Successful extemporaneous speakers use all of the tools available. Ineffective facial expressions take away two primary tools.

> No Facial Expression =
> No Vocal Expression

This is easy for those who are naturally expressive. For others, facial expressions require more work. One easy way to develop more facial expression is to use more stories in the speech. Everyone tends to be more expressive when sharing a good story. The facial expression that accompanies storytelling is commonly labeled *natural* facial expression. It tends to just happen when talking about something that engages emotions. Good extemporaneous speakers practice telling stories while looking in the mirror or videotaping themselves. As they watch themselves, they make note of how vocal expression follows facial expression. Then they can determine how to incorporate more facial expression into their speech.

Another form of facial expression is *overt* facial expression. This involves consciously deciding to make a specific expression for a specific situation. An example of this is to say, "That will make me really sad," followed by a pause where the speaker demonstrates a big frowning face. Overt facial expressions can be used for strong impact, but only when used sparingly. Audiences tend to become annoyed by them if they're overused.

Eyes are, of course, a part of the face. That partially explains why eye contact is one of the most critical components of effective public speaking. The additional opportunity for eye contact is arguably the greatest benefit of extemporaneous speaking. Since detailed notes or a manuscript are not needed, the speaker can maintain eye contact with the audience.

The phrase *eye contact* is itself instructive. Significant eye contact is the only way the audience knows that the speaker is really there. Without consistent eye contact, the speaker might as well be somewhere else. Speakers make contact with the audience through the eyes.

Eye contact is something that can be practiced during conversation. Research shows that listeners feel like there is usually a large deficit of eye contact on the part of the speaker even in interpersonal conversation.[2] That means the listener is trying to make eye contact much more often than the speaker. Audience members are unsure the speaker is genuine with them if they and the speaker do not make eye contact. Listeners will soon lose interest if speakers do not look at the audience. Effective extemporaneous speakers use interpersonal conversations to practice making eye contact. The practice carries over to better eye contact when speaking in public.

Public speakers who maintain good eye contact with the audience communicate a higher degree of integrity and confidence than those who consistently avoid looking audience members in the eye.

Strategies for eye contact will vary depending on the size of the audience. A small audience will necessitate having eye contact

SUSAN B. ANTHONY

Susan B. Anthony was born in 1820 into a Quaker family in Adams, Massachusetts. She was a teacher in early adulthood and later assisted with the family farm near Rochester, New York. She worked with several of the popular reform movements of the mid-nineteenth century, but is best known for her efforts on behalf of women's suffrage.

Anthony's work as a reformer led her to speak before large audiences across the United States. Her audiences included state legislatures, political conventions, and reform rallies. Concerning the earliest of these addresses, Katherine Anthony writes, "Susan was knocking on a door that she half dreaded to see opened. To demand that women be allowed to speak in public required of her the purest courage, for she was no speaker."[1]

Apparently Anthony never did gain confidence as a public speaker. In fact, an obituary of Anthony that appeared in a Des Moines, Iowa, newspaper declared, "Miss Anthony was not an orator, but her addresses did more for the advancement of women than those of a dozen women of her time."[2]

She did public speaking simply because the platform for her cause was available. "Before 1858 she tried to memorize or to speak from prepared manuscripts, and these samples seem stilted and labored. For the rest of her career she spoke from notes . . ."[3] The result was full participation in the public arena for half of the citizens of the United States.

NOTES

1. Katherine Anthony, *Susan B. Anthony: Her Personal History and Her Era* (New York: Russell and Russell, 1954), 111.
2. Ibid., 130.
3. Doris Yoakim Twichell, "Susan B. Anthony," *History and Criticism of American Public Address*, Vol. III, ed. Marie Kathryn Hochmuth, 97–132 (New York: McGraw-Hill, 1955), 114.

with everyone. This is the only way each member will feel like he or she is being engaged. With larger audiences, it's not necessary to have contact with everyone in order for members to feel like they are included. It's easier to make all members feel like they are receiving eye contact (even though they might not be) due to the fact that the angle of vision increases the farther away we are from the object of our gaze.

A mental picture of how angle of vision works is to imagine that someone you don't recognize is looking in your direction from the other side of a large room. She smiles and makes a gesture, motioning as if she wants you to come toward her. As you walk toward the person, someone else passes, walking more quickly toward the same person. At that point you realize that you were not the object of the person's gaze.

Understanding how angle of vision functions allows a speaker to gain an advantage in speaking situations. When speaking to large audiences, speakers can single out those audience members who appear to be engaged. They're the ones who are smiling, nodding, and exhibiting other positive forms of nonverbal communication. When a speaker does this with audience members that are at a great enough distance, the audience members around them all think the speaker is having eye contact with them as well. This allows a speaker to minimize the amount of time spent making real eye contact with those that appear less enthusiastic about what is being said. As a result, the speaker has more positive energy.

VOICE

In addition to physical appearance, movement, and facial expression as speaking tools, the most effective speakers consider the use of voice. Key elements to the use of the voice as a speaking tool include rhythm, level, quality, and clarity. Each of these components must be used effectively in order to engage the audience.

The rhythm of the voice is composed of pace, tempo, and pauses. Pace is the foundation and must be correct in order for the other two elements to work well. Pace is the overall rate at which the message is delivered. Pace must match the occasion, audience, and topic in order to be effective. For example, when telling a story about an exciting event, the pace should be a little quicker. But when delivering some sad news, the pace should be slower.

The second component of voice is the tempo. The tempo will vary depending on the tenor or mood of each section of the speech. The action of the speech also dictates the tempo. For example, the tempo will be quicker when talking about a tense, anxiety-filled situation. But if a portion of the speech is addressing a time of contemplative reflection, the tempo will be slower. Speakers generally use these reasons to govern the tempo, but at times it may be necessary to vary the tempo just to keep the audience engaged.

The final element of rhythm is the pause. Mark Twain said the pause is an exceedingly important point in any story. Some of the reasons that support this idea are related to the functions that the pause performs. The most common function is using a pause as a transition. It's much like fading to black in a film, or dimming the lights at a play. It indicates a change of time or setting. The pause can also be used for emphasis. Pausing before or after a key portion of a speech serves to set that portion apart as important. Creating suspense can be another effective result of the pause.

The level of the voice involves both volume and projection. Volume is how loud or soft the voice is. The tendency of beginning speakers is to overuse the loud side. This seems to be especially true in large audiences and can create communication problems between the speaker and the audience. Most audiences become tired of loud voices. One effective speaker was addressing a large and somewhat unruly audience. He took off his lapel microphone, held it just in front of his lips, and spoke in a soft voice. The soft voice can often be more powerful than the loud voice. This truth is evidenced by what happens in a noisy room when someone starts to whisper. In a short period of time people stop talking and strain to hear the whisper.

Projection is the force behind the voice. Effective projection involves control of the diaphragm and allows the audience to hear the speaker even when he or she is using low volume as a vocal tool. To accomplish this, there must be enough force behind the voice to push it to the back row so that all audience members can hear. A stage whisper used in a theatrical production would be a good example of the effective use of projection.

The third element to consider when using the voice as a speaking tool is the quality of the voice. Voice quality includes inflection and the tone of the voice. When used appropriately, these two elements convey the energy and mood of the speech.

Inflection is the high or low fluctuation of the voice. The key for successful use of this element is variation. When the voice remains at one level for too long, the dreaded monotone is the result. It brings to mind the "Wah, wah, wah, wah, wah" sound of the teacher's voice from Charlie Brown's cartoon classroom. Monotone voices express no energy.

Tone is the general tenor of the voice and is used to convey emotion. Tone is generally linked to a combination of tempo and inflection. For instance, excitement is indicated by using the high end of the voice in a quick manner, while sadness is indicated by speaking slowly and using the low end of the voice. Anger is often communicated by a choppy or halted sharpness.

The final element of the voice as a tool is clarity. Clarity is the result of articulation, pronunciation, and general vocal quality.

Articulation relates to the formation and sound of letters. Each letter should be given its correct sound. *T*'s and *D*'s are interdentals and must be articulated properly in order to help audience members tell the difference between the two. Saying, "it doesn't madder," instead of, "it doesn't matter," is an example of an articulation error.

Two additional articulation problems are letter dropping and letter adding. Both are just what the names indicate. New Englanders commonly drop the letter *R* from the end of words. An example would be how they say the name of one of their favorite foods: "I like lobstuh," instead of, "I like lobster." Similarly, an increasingly universal practice of letter dropping in American youth culture is to drop the *T* in the middle of words. They might say, "I lost my bu-on," instead of, "I lost my button." One might also hear, "The apple is ro-en," instead of, "The apple is rotten."

New Englanders also have a tendency to add the letter *R* to words that end with vowels. For instance, Lynda will say, "Hi, my name is Lynder, and I have a great idear." These are classic examples of letter adding.

Pronunciation is making sure that the emphasis is in the right place and that sound groupings are correct. Pronunciation should be unobtrusive. In his book *How to Make a Good Speech*, Leroy Brown says, "It should not attract attention to itself in any way."[3] There are many types of pronunciation errors. One common error is the adding of sounds. Another is subtracting sounds. Some speakers substitute one sound for another. An example of this is using *dem*, *dat*, *dese*, and *dose* instead of *them*, *that*, *these*, and *those*; or using *ax* when the intention is to say *ask*. Speakers will occasionally reverse sounds. Misplaced stresses create another common pronunciation error.

WORDS

Although the effective extemporaneous speaker does not work from a manuscript or a detailed outline, words remain vitally important. The extemporaneous speaker focuses on ideas, but not to the exclusion of words. That means that the focus should be on conveying a certain meaning rather than on a predetermined collection of words. Developing a solid core structure helps the speaker accomplish this. In every case, however, it's important to keep the structure simple and to build points that will be easy for the speaker and the audience to remember.

This means practicing key words that are going to be used. The key to word-usage preparation is attention to correct word choice. Denotation errors are those embarrassing scenarios in which a speaker will use a word inconsistent with its dictionary definition. Particularly problematic can be the use of malapropisms—denotation errors that are unintentionally humorous misuses or distortions of a word or phrase.

For instance, a speaker may intend to recount a journey in which he finally reaches the destination. But by using the word *destiny*, he communicates a more philosophical or even ominous message. Then there's the ever-popular denotation error of the word *literally*. Of course the actual meaning of this adverb is to communicate the opposite meaning of the word *figuratively*, rather than the common assumption that it means extremely or actually. For instance, when a soccer player says that his opponent, "Literally blew me away," we don't think it's literal—unless his opponent happens to be the big bad wolf.

Careful attention also needs to be given to the connotation of words. Connotation is the suggestive meaning of a word, apart from the thing it explicitly names or describes. For instance, while their denotations may be identical, the connotation of thin is quite different from skinny. Likewise, a careful speaker will not accidentally or unintentionally use the word *infamous* to humorously describe a local politician's policies. Audience members will undoubtedly interpret the word *infamous* as carrying negative connotations.

Words carry explicit and implicit meanings. It's important for speakers to be aware of their own vocabularies and not to rely upon an interpreted meaning that is based on a thesaurus listing, or how the word might have been employed in the context of a conversation, speech, or reading. The simplest protection against this common problem is a self-awareness that acknowledges, "I don't really know the exact meaning of this word," and a willingness to pull out the dictionary and research the word.

The best extemporaneous speakers have some key words and phrases that are carefully and attentively chosen ahead of time. These words give the audience hooks where they can hang the rest of the information.

Effective extemporaneous speakers must also consider the structure of their delivery notes. Notes for an extemporaneous speaker should be brief and prepared in a manner that does not cause the speaker to feel confined by them. Notes are a servant rather than a master of the effective speaker. Most of the issues related to notes are a matter of individual preference. Some speakers prefer typed notes while others prefer handwritten notes. Some speakers use particular spacing in the notes. Some also include delivery cues. The speaker needs to experiment in order to find what note system works best. Generally, notes should only fill the first two-thirds of the page so the speaker doesn't have to look down as far. If notes are on the last third of the page, eye contact becomes difficult.

The use of story or narrative is another aspect of the use of words that must be considered by the extemporaneous speaker. Stories and narratives free the speaker to have more eye contact and be more expressive.

Beginning extemporaneous speakers often raise questions about the level of detail to include in a story. The speaker must know both the details of the story and how much detail to include. Flexibility is important with the details. If the audience appears bored, the speaker needs to cull some of the detail. If the audience looks quizzical or pensive, the speaker needs to add detail. Since stories, and the points that they support, are generally easy for an audience to remember, extemporaneous speakers should use them liberally.

Since all speakers tend to be more animated and expressive when sharing stories, narratives provide a great opportunity for expression. Using stories provides the extemporaneous speaker with a good opportunity to use all the elements of body and voice discussed earlier. Since narratives tend to flow naturally, more focus can be placed on being strategic about the delivery.

Effective use of body, voice, and words are essential to effective extemporaneous delivery. Implementing the techniques discussed in each of these areas will provide an enjoyable speaking and listening experience for both the speaker and the audience. A speaker who utilizes them will become someone who totally captivates the attention of the audience.

5
CONCLUSION

After a careful examination of the advantages and challenges of extemporaneous delivery, it should be apparent why Elizabeth Dole chose this delivery method to address those present at the Republican National Convention on August 14, 1996. The impact of her speech demonstrates that she utilized the advantages and overcame the challenges of extemporaneous speaking through careful preparation and effective delivery.

Whether you are a seasoned speaker or a beginning student of public speaking and homiletics, you can deliver speeches that achieve the results you desire just as Elizabeth Dole did. Implementing the strategies and techniques discussed in *Brief Guide to Extemporaneous Public Speaking* allows every speaker to create a deft and commanding performance that will capture and maintain audience attention.

Whenever possible, accept the challenge to speak extemporaneously. Never let fear be a factor. Be so busy communicating that you forget to be afraid. Keep your mind focused on being your best for every audience. Each time you begin a speech, you should say to yourself, "Sitting before me are the best people in the world. Therefore they deserve my best."[1] That best involves planned and practiced extemporaneous delivery.

NOTES

INTRODUCTION

1. Steven E. Lucas, *The Art of Public Speaking*, 9th ed. (New York: McGraw-Hill, 2007), 304.

2. Curt Anderson, "Dole Family Touts Their Favorite: Candidate's Wife Spreads Message Among Delegates at GOP Convention," *Rocky Mountain News* (August 15, 1996), section 1.

3. Adam Nagourney, "Dole Follows in Footsteps of Wife, Who Stars Again," *New York Times* (August 16, 1996), section A.

4. Richard L. Weaver II, *Essentials of Public Speaking*, 2nd ed. (Boston: Allyn and Bacon, 2001), 178.

5. Lucas, 78.

1. ADVANTAGES OF EXTEMPORANEOUS DELIVERY

1. The speech can be viewed online at americanrhetoric.com or is available on CD or videocassette. *Greatest Speeches: The Video Series*, Vol. I. (Greenwood, Ind.: Educational Video Group).

2. See for example: Em Grifffin, *A First Look at Communication Theory*, 3rd ed. (New York: McGraw-Hill, 1997), 304–311. See also Alexandra Alvarez, "Martin Luther King's 'I Have a Dream': The Speech Event as Metaphor," *Journal of Black Studies* 18, no. 3 (1988): 337–57.

3. Steven E. Lucas, *The Art of Public Speaking*, 9th ed. (New York: McGraw-Hill, 2007), A-7.

4. Mervyn A. Warren, *King Came Preaching: The Pulpit Power of Dr. Martin Luther King Jr.* (Downers Grove, Ill.: InterVarsity, 2001), 158.

5. Wayne V. McDill, *The Moment of Truth* (Nashville: Broadman, 1999), 137.
6. Doris Yoakam Twichell, "Susan B. Anthony," *History and Criticism of American Public Address*, Vol. III, ed. Marie Kathryn Hochmuth (New York: McGraw-Hill, 1955), 97–132.

2. CHALLENGES TO EXTEMPORANEOUS DELIVERY

1. Kevin Cowherd, "Speaking in Public: No Scarier than Flying," *Fort Wayne Journal Gazette* (December 23, 1989), Section A.
2. Sherry Devereaux Ferguson, *Public Speaking: Building Competency in Stages* (New York: Oxford, 2008), 162.

3. PREPARING AN EXTEMPORANEOUS SPEECH

1. Steven Levy, "The World According to Google," *Newsweek* (December 16, 2002), 46–51.
2. Randolph Hock, *The Extreme Searcher's Guide to Web Search Engines: A Handbook for the Serious Researcher*, 2nd ed. (Medford, N.J.: Information Today, 2001).
3. See for example Robert A. Traina, *Methodical Bible Study* (Grand Rapids: Zondervan, 1980) or Gordon D. Fee and Douglas K. Stuart, *How to Read the Bible for All It's Worth* (Grand Rapids: Zondervan, 2003).
4. Edward J. Golob and Arnold Starr, "Serial Position Effects in Auditory Event: Related Potentials During Working Memory Retrieval," *Journal of Cognitive Neuroscience* 16, no. 1 (2004), 40–53.
5. Kerstin H. Seiler and Johannes Engelkamp, "The Role of Item-Specific Information for the Serial Position Curve in Free Recall," *Journal of Experimental Psychology: Learning, Memory and Cognition* 29, no. 5 (2003): 954–65.
6. Deanna D. Sellnow, *Confident Public Speaking*, 2nd ed. (Bellmont, Calif.: Thomson Wadsworth, 2005), 202.
7. Steven E. Lucas, *The Art of Public Speaking*, 9th ed. (New York: McGraw-Hill, 2007), 247.
8. Bert Decker, *The Art of Communicating* (Oakville, Ontario: Reid, 1988).

4. DELIVERING AN EXTEMPORANEOUS SPEECH

1. See Judson Mills and Elliot Aronson, "Opinion Change as a Function of the Communicator's Attractiveness and Desire to Influence," *Journal of Personality and Social Psychology* 1 (1965), 73–77. See also R. N. Widgery and B. Webster, "The Effects of Physical Attractiveness upon Perceived Initial Credibility," *Michigan Speech Association Journal* 4 (1969): 9–15.
2. C. Goodwin, *Conversational Organization: Interaction between Speakers and Hearers* (New York: Academic Press, 1981).
3. Leroy Brown, *How to Make a Good Speech* (New York: Frederick Fell, 1962), 68.

5. CONCLUSION

1. Leroy Brown, *How to Make a Good Speech* (New York: Frederick Fell, 1962), 13.